READING POWER

School Newspaper

Rae Emmer

The Rosen Publishing Group's
PowerKids Press™
New York

Published in 2002 by The Rosen Publishing Group, Inc.
29 East 21st Street, New York, NY 10010

First Edition

Book Design: Christopher Logan

Photo Credits: Maura Boruchow

Emmer, Rae.
    School newspaper / by Rae Emmer.
        p. cm.— (School activities)
    Includes bibliographical references and index.
    Summary: This book describes the work that is involved in creating a school newspaper, including writing stories, taking pictures, and putting the paper together.
    ISBN 0-8239-5966-X
    1. Student newspapers and periodicals—Juvenile literature. [1. Newspapers. 2. Journalism.] I. Title. II. Series.
    2002
371.8'974—dc21

Manufactured in the United States of America

Contents

School Newspaper

We have a school newspaper. The teacher helps us make the newspaper.

We have to work together to make the newspaper.

Writing Stories

We write stories for the paper.

We ask other students questions for our stories.

We also take pictures to go with our stories.

13

Putting the Paper Together

We work on the computer to make the paper. We put the stories and the pictures together.

Then we all put the pages of the paper together.

Our friends like to read the paper.

We are proud of our work.

Glossary

computer (kuhm-**pyoo**-tuhr) an electronic machine that stores and recalls information

newspaper (**nooz**-pay-puhr) a paper that tells the news

proud (**prowd**) feeling pleased with what you have done

stories (**stor**-eez) reports of things that have happened

Resources

Books
Deadline!: From News to Newspaper
by Gail Gibbons
HarperCollins Children's Books (1987)

The Young Journalist's Book: How to Write and Produce Your Own Newspaper
by Nancy Bentley and Donna Guthrie
Millbrook Press (2000)

Web Site
http://www.kidsreport.com

Index

Word Count: 84

Note to Librarians, Teachers, and Parents

If reading is a challenge, Reading Power is a solution! Reading Power is perfect for readers who want high-interest subject matter at an accessible reading level. These fact-filled, photo-illustrated books are designed for readers who want straightforward vocabulary, engaging topics, and a manageable reading experience. With clear picture/text correspondence, leveled Reading Power books put the reader in charge. Now readers have the power to get the information they want and the skills they need in a user-friendly format.